D0319622

# The Usborne Book of Poetry

# The Usborne Book of Poetry

Collected by Sam Taplin

Illustrated by Kristina Swarner

Designed by Matt Durber

# Contents

When I was about twelve years old, I picked up a book of poetry and leafed through it. It fell open and I read the poem that was printed on that page. I can still remember how I felt as I got to the end – it was as though something had jumped out of the innocent book that had been sitting on the shelf, something beautiful and surprising and strange.

I snapped the book shut and after a few
seconds I opened it again in the same
place – this time I was prepared so I knew
the poem wouldn't be able to catch me out.
But it did, again. And it still does now.

I don't know how poems do this. They're
just a few lines of words arranged so that
they have a rhythm and (sometimes) rhymes,
but when you read a good one it can be so
exciting that you never forget it. Be careful
when you open this book – it's stuffed with
poems waiting to ambush you.

Some of the poems are funny, and some
are sad, and some will make you feel exactly
how the poet felt at a particular moment long,
long ago. They've been making my life a more
extraordinary place to be for quite a while
now. I hope they do the same for you.

Sam Taplin

# The Way Through the Woods

They shut the road through the woods
Seventy years ago.
Weather and rain have undone it again,
And now you would never know
There was once a road through the woods
Before they planted the trees.
It is underneath the coppice and heath
And the thin anemones.
Only the keeper sees
That, where the ring-dove broods,
And the badgers roll at ease,
There was once a road through the woods.

Yet, if you enter the woods
Of a summer evening late,
When the night-air cools on the trout-ringed pools
Where the otter whistles his mate,
(They fear not men in the woods,
Because they see so few.)
You will hear the beat of a horse's feet,
And the swish of a skirt in the dew,
Steadily cantering through
The misty solitudes,
As though they perfectly knew
The old lost road through the woods...
But there is no road through the woods.

Rudyard Kipling

# It was a Lover and his Lass

It was a lover and his lass,
   With a hey, and a ho, and a hey nonino,
That o'er the green cornfield did pass,
   In springtime, the only pretty ring time,
When birds do sing, hey ding a ding, ding;
Sweet lovers love the spring.

Between the acres of the rye,
   With a hey, and a ho, and a hey nonino,
Those pretty country folks would lie,
   In springtime, the only pretty ring time,
When birds do sing, hey ding a ding, ding;
Sweet lovers love the spring.

This carol they began that hour,
   With a hey, and a ho, and a hey nonino,
How that a life was but a flower
   In springtime, the only pretty ring time,
When birds do sing, hey ding a ding, ding;
Sweet lovers love the spring.

And therefore take the present time,
   With a hey, and a ho, and a hey nonino;
For love is crownèd with the prime
   In springtime, the only pretty ring time,
When birds do sing, hey ding a ding, ding;
Sweet lovers love the spring.

William Shakespeare

# Daffodils

I wandered lonely as a cloud
That floats on high o'er vales and hills,
When all at once I saw a crowd,
A host, of golden daffodils;
Beside the lake, beneath the trees,
Fluttering and dancing in the breeze.

Continuous as the stars that shine
And twinkle on the Milky Way,
They stretched in never-ending line
Along the margin of a bay:
Ten thousand saw I at a glance,
Tossing their heads in sprightly dance.

The waves beside them danced, but they
Out-did the sparkling waves in glee.
A poet could not but be gay,
In such a jocund company:
I gazed – and gazed – but little thought
What wealth the show to me had brought.

For oft, when on my couch I lie
In vacant or in pensive mood,
They flash upon that inward eye
Which is the bliss of solitude;
And then my heart with pleasure fills,
And dances with the daffodils.

William Wordsworth

# The Purist

I give you now Professor Twist,
A conscientious scientist,
Trustees exclaimed, "He never bungles!"
And sent him off to distant jungles.
Camped on a tropic riverside,
One day he missed his loving bride.
She had, the guide informed him later,
Been eaten by an alligator.
Professor Twist could not but smile.
"You mean," he said, "a crocodile."

Ogden Nash

# Song Sung by a Man on a Barge to Another Man on a Different Barge in order to Drive him Mad

Oh,

I am the best bargee bar none,
You are the best bargee bar one!
You are the second-best bargee,
You are the best bargee bar me!

Oh,

I am the best...

(and so on, until he is
*hurled into the canal*)

Kit Wright

# Moonlit Apples

At the top of the house the apples are laid in rows,
And the skylight lets the moonlight in, and those
Apples are deep-sea apples of green. There goes
  A cloud on the moon in the autumn night.

A mouse in the wainscot scratches, and scratches, and then
There is no sound at the top of the house of men
Or mice; and the cloud is blown, and the moon again
  Dapples the apples with deep-sea light.

They are lying in rows there, under the gloomy beams;
On the sagging floor; they gather the silver streams
Out of the moon, those moonlit apples of dreams,
  And quiet is the steep stair under.

In the corridors under there is nothing but sleep.
And stiller than ever on orchard boughs they keep
Tryst with the moon, and deep is the silence, deep
  On moon-washed apples of wonder.

John Drinkwater

# The Day that Summer Died

From all around the mourners came
  The day that Summer died,
From hill and valley, field and wood
  And lake and mountainside.

They did not come in funeral black
  But every mourner chose
Gorgeous colours or soft shades
  Of russet, yellow, rose.

18

Horse chestnut, oak and sycamore
    Wore robes of gold and red;
The rowan sported scarlet beads;
    No bitter tears were shed;

Although at dusk the mourners heard,
    As a small wind softly sighed,
A touch of sadness in the air
    The day that Summer died.

Vernon Scannell

# The Hen

The Hen is a ferocious fowl,
She pecks you till she makes you howl.

And all the time she flaps her wings,
And says the most insulting things.

And when you try to take her eggs,
She bites large pieces from your legs.

The only safe way to get these,
Is to creep on your hands and knees.

In the meanwhile a friend must hide,
And jump out on the other side.

And then you snatch the eggs and run,
While she pursues the other one.

The difficulty is, to find
A trusty friend who will not mind.

Lord Alfred Douglas

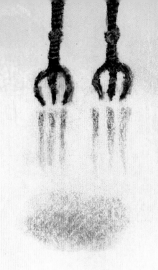

# The Duck

I hope you may have better luck
Than to be bitten by the Duck.

This bird is generally tame,
But he is dangerous all the same;

And though he looks so small and weak,
He has a very powerful beak.

Between the hours of twelve and two
You never know what he may do.

And sometimes he plays awkward tricks
From half-past four to half-past six.

And any hour of the day
It's best to keep out of his way.

Lord Alfred Douglas

# The Nonny

The Nonny-bird I love particularly;
All day she chirps her joysome odes.
She rises perpendicularly,
And if she goes too far, explodes.

James Reeves

# Stopping by Woods on a Snowy Evening

Whose woods these are I think I know.
His house is in the village though;
He will not see me stopping here
To watch his woods fill up with snow.

My little horse must think it queer
To stop without a farmhouse near
Between the woods and frozen lake
The darkest evening of the year.

He gives his harness bells a shake
To ask if there is some mistake.
The only other sound's the sweep
Of easy wind and downy flake.

The woods are lovely, dark and deep,
But I have promises to keep,
And miles to go before I sleep,
And miles to go before I sleep.

Robert Frost

# Snow in the Suburbs

Every branch big with it,
Bent every twig with it;
Every fork like a white web-foot;
Every street and pavement mute:
Some flakes have lost their way, and grope back upward, when
Meeting those meandering down they turn and descend again.
The palings are glued together like a wall,
And there is no waft of wind with the fleecy fall.

A sparrow enters the tree,
Whereon immediately
A snow-lump thrice his own slight size
Descends on him and showers his head and eyes,
And overturns him,
And near inurns him,
And lights on a nether twig, when its brush
Starts off a volley of other lodging lumps with a rush.

The steps are a blanched slope,
Up which, with feeble hope,
A black cat comes, wide-eyed and thin;
And we take him in.

Thomas Hardy

23

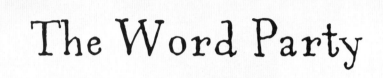

# The Word Party

Loving words clutch crimson roses,
Rude words sniff and pick their noses,
Sly words come dressed up as foxes,
Short words stand on cardboard boxes,
Common words tell jokes and gabble,
Complicated words play Scrabble,
Swear words stamp around and shout,
Hard words stare each other out,
Foreign words look lost and shrug,
Careless words trip on the rug,
Long words slouch with stooping shoulders,
Code words carry secret folders,
Silly words flick rubber bands,
Hyphenated words hold hands,
Strong words show off, bending metal,
Sweet words call each other "petal",
Small words yawn and suck their thumbs
Till at last the morning comes.
Kind words give out farewell posies…

Snap! The dictionary closes.

Richard Edwards

# Words I Like

Billowing, seaboard, ocean, pearl,
Estuary, shale, maroon;
Harlequin, runnel, ripple, swirl,
Labyrinth, lash, lagoon.

Razorbill, cygnet, songbird, kite,
Cormorant, crag, ravine;
Flickering, sun-burst, dappled, flight,
Fiery, dew, serene.

Asteroid, nova, stardust, moon,
Galaxy, zone, eclipse;
Dynamo, pulsar, planet, rune,
Satellite, spangle, lips.

Boulevard, freeway, turnpike, cruise,
Chevrolet, fin, pavanne;
Tomahawk, firecrest, fantail, fuse,
Saskatchewan, Sioux, Cheyenne.

Tenderness, sweetheart, cherish, miss,
Paramour, fond, befriend;
Affection, cosy, cuddle, kiss,
Family, love, the end.

Steve Turner

# The Magic Box

I will put in the box

the swish of a silk sari on a summer night,
fire from the nostrils of a Chinese dragon,
the top of a tongue touching a tooth.

I will put in the box

a snowman with a rumbling belly,
a sip of the bluest water from Lake Lucerne,
a leaping spark from an electric fish.

I will put in the box

three violet wishes spoken in Gujarati,
the last joke of an ancient uncle
and the first smile of a baby.

I will put in the box

a fifth season and a black sun,
a cowboy on a broomstick
and a witch on a white horse.

My box is fashioned from ice and gold and steel,
with stars on the lid and secrets in the corners.
Its hinges are the toe joints
of dinosaurs.

I shall surf on my box
on the great high-rolling breaks of the wild Atlantic,
then wash ashore on a yellow beach
the colour of the sun.

Kit Wright

# Out in the Desert

Out in the desert lies the sphinx

It never eats and it never drinx

Its body quite solid without any chinx

And when the sky's all purples and pinx

(As if it was painted with coloured inx)

And the sun it ever so swiftly sinx

Behind the hills in a couple of twinx

You may hear (if you're lucky) a bell that clinx

And also tolls and also tinx

And they say at the very same sound the sphinx

It sometimes smiles and it sometimes winx.


But nobody knows just what it thinx.


Charles Causley

# An April Sunday Brings the Snow

An April Sunday brings the snow
Making the blossom on the plum trees green,
Not white. An hour or two, and it will go.
Strange that I spend that hour moving between

Cupboard and cupboard, shifting the store
Of jam you made of fruit from these same trees:
Five loads – a hundred pounds or more –
More than enough for all next summer's teas,

Which now you will not sit and eat.
Behind the glass, under the cellophane,
Remains your final summer – sweet
And meaningless, and not to come again.

Philip Larkin

# The Cod

There's something very strange and odd
About the habits of the Cod.

For when you're swimming in the sea,
He sometimes bites you on the knee.

And though his bites are not past healing,
It is a most unpleasant feeling.

And when you're diving down below,
He often nips you on the toe.

And though he doesn't hurt you much,
He has a disagreeable touch.

There's one thing to be said for him –
It is a treat to see him swim.

But though he swims in graceful curves,
He rather gets upon your nerves.

Lord Alfred Douglas

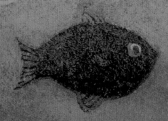

# The Emergensea

The octopus awoke one morning and wondered what rhyme it was.
 Looking at his alarm-clocktopus
  he saw that it had stopped
  and it was time to stop having a rest
  and get himself dressed.
  On every octofoot
 he put
 an octosocktopus
but in his hurry, one foot got put
not into an octosock
 but into an electric plug socket
  and the octopus got a nasty electric shocktopus
  and had to call the octodoctopus
   who couldn't get in
   to give any help or medicine
   because the door was loctopus.
   The octopus couldn't move, being in a state of octoshocktopus
   so the octodoctopus bashed the door
   to the floor
  and the cure was as simple as could be:
 a nice refreshing cup of
seawater.

John Hegley

# The Table and the Chair

Said the Table to the Chair,
"You can hardly be aware,
How I suffer from the heat
And from chilblains on my feet!
If we took a little walk,
We might have a little talk!
Pray let us take the air!"
Said the Table to the Chair.

Said the Chair unto the Table,
"Now you *know* we are not able!
How foolishly you talk,
When you know we *cannot* walk!"
Said the Table, with a sigh,
"It can do no harm to try,
I've as many legs as you,
Why can't we walk on two?"

So they both went slowly down,
And walked about the town
With a cheerful bumpy sound,
As they toddled round and round.
And everybody cried,
As they hastened to their side,
"See! the Table and the Chair
Have come out to take the air!"

But in going down an alley,
To a castle in a valley,
They completely lost their way,
And wandered all the day,
Till, to see them safely back,
They paid a Ducky-quack,
And a Beetle, and a Mouse,
Who took them to their house.

Then they whispered to each other,
"O delightful little brother!
What a lovely walk we've taken!
Let us dine on Beans and Bacon!"
So the Ducky, and the leetle
Browny-Mousy and the Beetle
Dined, and danced upon their heads
Till they toddled to their beds.

Edward Lear

# Geography Lesson

Our teacher told us one day he would leave
And sail across a warm blue sea
To places he had only known from maps,
And all his life had longed to be.

The house he lived in was narrow and grey
But in his mind's eye he could see
Sweet-scented jasmine clinging to the walls,
And green leaves burning on an orange tree.

He spoke of the lands he longed to visit,
Where it was never drab or cold.
I couldn't understand why he never left,
And shook off the school's stranglehold.

Then halfway through his final term
He took ill and never returned.
He never got to that place on the map
Where the green leaves of the orange trees burned.

The maps were redrawn on the classroom wall;
His name forgotten, he faded away.
But a lesson he never knew he taught
Is with me to this day.

I travel to where the green leaves burn,
To where the ocean's glass-clear and blue,
To places our teacher taught me to love –
And which he never knew.

Brian Patten

# A Smuggler's Song

If you wake at midnight, and hear a horse's feet,
Don't go drawing back the blind, or looking in the street,
Them that asks no questions isn't told a lie.
Watch the wall, my darling, while the Gentlemen go by!
     Five and twenty ponies,
     Trotting through the dark –
     Brandy for the Parson,
     'Baccy for the Clerk;
     Laces for a lady, letters for a spy,
And watch the wall, my darling, while the Gentlemen go by!

Running round the woodlump if you chance to find
Little barrels, roped and tarred, all full of brandy-wine,
Don't you shout to come and look, nor take 'em for your play.
Put the brushwood back again – and they'll be gone next day!

If you see the stable-door setting open wide;
If you see a tired horse lying down inside;
If your mother mends a coat cut about and tore;
If the lining's wet and warm – don't you ask no more!

If you meet King George's men, dressed in blue and red,
You be careful what you say, and mindful what is said.
If they call you "pretty maid", and chuck you 'neath the chin,
Don't you tell where no one is, nor yet where no one's been!

Knocks and footsteps round the house – whistles after dark –
You've no call for running out till the house-dogs bark.
*Trusty*'s here, and *Pincher*'s here, and see how dumb they lie –
*They* don't fret to follow when the Gentlemen go by!

If you do as you've been told, likely there's a chance,
You'll be give a dainty doll, all the way from France,
With a cap of Valenciennes, and a velvet hood –
A present from the Gentlemen, along o' being good!
     Five and twenty ponies,
     Trotting through the dark –
     Brandy for the Parson,
     'Baccy for the Clerk;
Them that asks no questions isn't told a lie –
Watch the wall, my darling, while the Gentlemen go by!

Rudyard Kipling

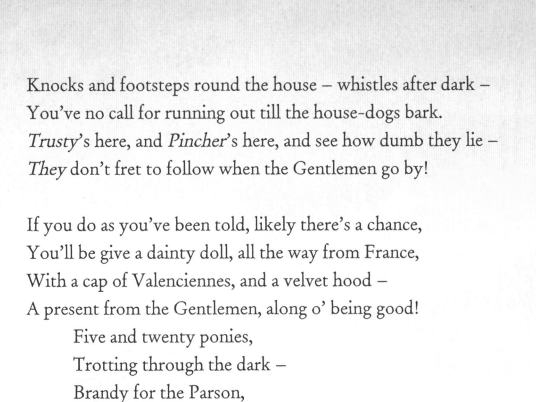

# A Small Dragon

I've found a small dragon in the woodshed.
Think it must have come from deep inside a forest
because it's damp and green and leaves
are still reflecting in its eyes.

I fed it on many things, tried grass,
the roots of stars, hazel-nut and dandelion,
but it stared up at me as if to say, I need
foods you can't provide.

It made a nest among the coal,
not unlike a bird's but larger,
it is out of place here
and is quite silent.

If you believed in it I would come
hurrying to your house to let you share my wonder,
but I want instead to see
if you yourself will pass this way.

Brian Patten

# The Adventures of Isabel

Isabel met an enormous bear,
Isabel, Isabel, didn't care;
The bear was hungry, the bear was ravenous,
The bear's big mouth was cruel and cavernous.
The bear said, Isabel, glad to meet you,
How do, Isabel, now I'll eat you!
Isabel, Isabel, didn't worry,
Isabel didn't scream or scurry.
She washed her hands and she straightened her hair up,
Then Isabel quietly ate the bear up.

Once in a night as black as pitch
Isabel met a wicked old witch.
The witch's face was cross and wrinkled,
The witch's gums with teeth were sprinkled.
Ho ho, Isabel! the old witch crowed,
I'll turn you into an ugly toad!
Isabel, Isabel, didn't worry,
Isabel didn't scream or scurry,
She showed no rage and she showed no rancour,
But she turned the witch into milk and drank her.

Isabel met a hideous giant,
Isabel continued self-reliant.
The giant was hairy, the giant was horrid,
He had one eye in the middle of his forehead.
Good morning, Isabel, the giant said,
I'll grind your bones to make my bread.
Isabel, Isabel, didn't worry,
Isabel didn't scream or scurry.
She nibbled the zwieback that she always fed off,
And when it was gone, she cut the giant's head off.

Isabel met a troublesome doctor,
He punched and he poked till he really shocked her.
The doctor's talk was of coughs and chills
And the doctor's satchel bulged with pills.
The doctor said unto Isabel,
Swallow this, it will make you well.
Isabel, Isabel, didn't worry,
Isabel didn't scream or scurry.
She took those pills from the pill concocter,
And Isabel calmly cured the doctor.

Ogden Nash

# Mountains

Mountains are today, yesterday, and for ever.
They have no likes or dislikes, no opinions, –
But moods, yes. Their moods change like the weather.
They argue and quarrel, loud
With angry thunder. They rain
Rivers of stinging tears.
They hide their sulky heads in cloud
For days and days. Then suddenly, all smiles again,
One by one
Their magic cliffs stand clear
And brave, above a sea of white wave,
Under the lighthouse of the sun.

Ian Serraillier

44

# Eldorado

Gaily bedight,
A gallant knight,
In sunshine and in shadow,
Had journeyed long,
Singing a song,
In search of Eldorado.

But he grew old –
This knight so bold –
And o'er his heart a shadow
Fell as he found
No spot of ground
That looked like Eldorado.

And, as his strength
Failed him at length,
He met a pilgrim shadow:
"Shadow," said he,
"Where can it be,
This land of Eldorado?"

"Over the mountains
Of the Moon,
Down the valley of the Shadow,
Ride, boldly ride,"
The shade replied,
"If you seek for Eldorado."

Edgar Allan Poe

# Limerick

A limerick's cleverly versed —
The second line rhymes with the first;
The third one is short,
The fourth's the same sort,
And the last line is often the worst.

John Irwin

# There was a Young Bard of Japan

There was a young bard of Japan,
Whose limericks never would scan;
When told it was so,
He said: "Yes, I know,
But I always try and get as many words into the last line as I possibly can.

Anon

# Rather Perplexed

You may find yourself rather perplexed
By this poem. But if you get vexed,
Please abandon your rage,
For, without it, this page
Would be terribly lacking in text.

Pam Starling

# Clerihew

Jane Austen
Got lost in
Stoke-on-Trent.
Moral: She shouldn't have went.

Roger McGough

# from Exposure

Our brains ache, in the merciless iced east winds that knive us…
Wearied we keep awake because the night is silent…
Low, drooping flares confuse our memory of the salient…
Worried by silence, sentries whisper, curious, nervous,
    But nothing happens.

Watching, we hear the mad gusts tugging on the wire,
Like twitching agonies of men among its brambles.
Northward, incessantly, the flickering gunnery rumbles,
Far off, like a dull rumour of some other war.
    What are we doing here?

The poignant misery of dawn begins to grow...
We only know war lasts, rain soaks, and clouds sag stormy.
Dawn massing in the east her melancholy army
Attacks once more in ranks on shivering ranks of gray,
    But nothing happens.

Sudden successive flights of bullets streak the silence.
Less deadly than the air that shudders black with snow,
With sidelong flowing flakes that flock, pause, and renew,
We watch them wandering up and down the wind's nonchalance,
    But nothing happens.

Wilfred Owen

# The Fairies

Up the airy mountain,
Down the rushy glen,
We daren't go a-hunting
For fear of little men;
Wee folk, good folk,
Trooping all together;
Green jacket, red cap,
And white owl's feather!

Down along the rocky shore
Some make their home;
They live on crispy pancakes
Of yellow tide-foam;
Some in the reeds
Of the black mountain lake,
With frogs for their watch-dogs,
All night awake.

High on the hill-top
The old King sits;
He is now so old and grey
He's nigh lost his wits.

With a bridge of white mist
Columbkill he crosses,
On his stately journeys
From Slieveleague to Rosses;
Or going up with music
On cold starry nights,
To sup with the Queen
Of the gay Northern Lights.

They stole little Bridget
For seven years long;
When she came down again,
Her friends were all gone.

They took her lightly back,
Between the night and morrow,
They thought that she was fast asleep,
But she was dead with sorrow.
They have kept her ever since
Deep within the lake,
On a bed of flag-leaves,
Watching till she wake.

By the craggy hill-side,
Through the mosses bare,
They have planted thorn-trees
For pleasure here and there.
Is any man so daring
As dig them up in spite,
He shall find the thornies set
In his bed at night.

Up the airy mountain,
Down the rushy glen,
We daren't go a-hunting
For fear of little men;
Wee folk, good folk,
Trooping all together;
Green jacket, red cap,
And white owl's feather!

William Allingham

# The Uncertainty of the Poet

I am a poet.
I am very fond of bananas.

I am bananas.
I am very fond of a poet.

I am a poet of bananas.
I am very fond.

A fond poet of "I am, I am" –
Very bananas.

Fond of "Am I bananas?
Am I?" – a very poet.

Bananas of a poet!
Am I fond? Am I very?

Poet bananas! I am.
I am fond of a "very".

I am of very fond bananas.
Am I a poet?

Wendy Cope

# Flowers

Some men never think of it.
You did. You'd come along
And say you'd nearly brought me flowers
But something had gone wrong.

The shop was closed. Or you had doubts –
The sort that minds like ours
Dream up incessantly. You thought
I might not want your flowers.

It made me smile and hug you then.
Now I can only smile.
But, look, the flowers you nearly brought
Have lasted all this while.

Wendy Cope

# You are Old, Father William

"You are old, Father William," the young man said,
"And your hair has become very white;
And yet you incessantly stand on your head –
Do you think, at your age, it is right?"

"In my youth," Father William replied to his son,
"I feared it might injure the brain;
But, now that I'm perfectly sure I have none,
Why, I do it again and again."

"You are old," said the youth, "as I mentioned before,
And have grown most uncommonly fat;
Yet you turned a back-somersault in at the door –
Pray, what is the reason of that?"

"In my youth," said the sage, as he shook his grey locks,
"I kept all my limbs very supple
By the use of this ointment – one shilling the box –
Allow me to sell you a couple?"

"You are old," said the youth, "and your jaws are too weak
For anything tougher than suet;
Yet you finished the goose, with the bones and the beak –
Pray, how did you manage to do it?"

"In my youth," said his father, "I took to the law,
And argued each case with my wife;
And the muscular strength, which it gave to my jaw,
Has lasted the rest of my life."

"You are old," said the youth, "one would hardly suppose
That your eye was as steady as ever;
Yet you balanced an eel on the end of your nose –
What made you so awfully clever?"

"I have answered three questions, and that is enough,"
Said his father. "Don't give yourself airs!
Do you think I can listen all day to such stuff?
Be off, or I'll kick you downstairs!"

Lewis Carroll

# Night Football with my Brother

Our boys had won – we had to run and roar,

And so we charged, unseeing, to our pitch,

And dashed about like lunatics, to score

The winning goal again, to play the match.

We hardly felt the rising chill of night,

Too busy making angles in the blue

Day's end, my trainers quickened by the thought:

This is the closest I will get to you,

The clearest that you'll let yourself become.

Soon we only sensed each other's steps,

And stumbled over branches in the gloom,

And yet we sprinted on, our mute reflex

Ensuring that the struck ball never strayed.

And, though you're still a self-made mystery,

I knew then that a promise had been played,

That you would always pass it back to me.

We kept on punting passes through the dark;

They hurtled high and straight and glorious,

Keeping us apart across the park,

Smashing back and forth our tenderness.


Sam Taplin

# A Liking for the Viking

I've always had a liking for the Viking;
His handsome horns; his rough and ready ways;
His rugged russet hair beneath his helmet
In those metal-rattle, battle-happy days.

I've always had a longing for a longboat;
To fly like a dragon through the sea
To peaceful evenings round a real fire,
Alive with legend, rich with poetry.

I've always had a yearning for the burning
Of brave flames irradiating valour;
For the fiery longboat carrying its Chieftain
To his final feast in glorious Valhalla.

Celia Warren

# Roman Invasions

**BC55**

Julius Caesar,
Roman geezer,
Came to Britain,
Wasn't smitten,
Back to Gaul
After all.

**AD43**

Emperor Claudius,
More maraudius,
Had his reasons,
Sent more legions.
They were stronger,
Stayed much longer,
Long enough
For roads and stuff,
Built some baths,
Had some laughs,
England greener
Greater, Cleaner!

Celia Warren

# The Tiger

Tiger! Tiger! burning bright
In the forests of the night,
What immortal hand or eye
Could frame thy fearful symmetry?

In what distant deeps or skies
Burned the fire of thine eyes?
On what wings dare he aspire?
What the hand dare seize the fire?

And what shoulder, and what art,
Could twist the sinews of thy heart?
And when thy heart began to beat,
What dread hand? And what dread feet?

What the hammer? What the chain?
In what furnace was thy brain?
What the anvil? What dread grasp
Dare its deadly terrors clasp?

When the stars threw down their spears,
And watered heaven with their tears,
Did he smile his work to see?
Did he who made the Lamb make thee?

Tiger! Tiger! burning bright
In the forests of the night,
What immortal hand or eye
Dare frame thy fearful symmetry?

William Blake

# from
# The Lady of Shalott

On either side the river lie
Long fields of barley and of rye,
That clothe the wold and meet the sky;
And through the field the road runs by
      To many-towered Camelot;
And up and down the people go,
Gazing where the lilies blow
Round an island there below,
      The island of Shalott.

Willows whiten, aspens quiver,
Little breezes dusk and shiver
Through the wave that runs for ever
By the island in the river
      Flowing down to Camelot.
Four grey walls, and four grey towers,
Overlook a space of flowers,
And the silent isle imbowers
      The Lady of Shalott.

Only reapers, reaping early
In among the bearded barley,
Hear a song that echoes cheerly
From the river winding clearly,
        Down to towered Camelot:
And by the moon the reaper weary,
Piling sheaves in uplands airy,
Listening, whispers " 'Tis the fairy
        Lady of Shalott."

There she weaves by night and day
A magic web with colours gay.
She has heard a whisper say,
A curse is on her if she stay
        To look down to Camelot.
She knows not what the curse may be,
And so she weaveth steadily,
And little other care hath she,
        The Lady of Shalott.

And moving through a mirror clear
That hangs before her all the year,
Shadows of the world appear.
There she sees the highway near
     Winding down to Camelot:
There the river eddy whirls,
And there the surly village-churls,
And the red cloaks of market girls,
     Pass onward from Shalott.

All in the blue unclouded weather
Thick-jewelled shone the saddle-leather,
The helmet and the helmet-feather
Burned like one burning flame together,
     As he rode down to Camelot.
As often through the purple night,
Below the starry clusters bright,
Some bearded meteor, trailing light,
     Moves over still Shalott.

His broad clear brow in sunlight glowed;
On burnished hooves his war-horse trode;
From underneath his helmet flowed
His coal-black curls as on he rode,
     As he rode down to Camelot.
From the bank and from the river
He flashed into the crystal mirror,
"Tirra lirra," by the river
     Sang Sir Lancelot.

She left the web, she left the loom,
She made three paces through the room,
She saw the water-lily bloom,
She saw the helmet and the plume,
     She looked down to Camelot.
Out flew the web and floated wide;
The mirror cracked from side to side;
"The curse is come upon me," cried
     The Lady of Shalott.

Alfred Tennyson

# Look Back
# in Wonder

Though the Elephant's behind
Is delightfully designed
And the rump of any Rhino's mighty fine,
Though the buttocks of a Bear
Are indubitably fair
And the Pig is fundamentally divine,
Though the bum of any Bison
Is a singularly nice un,
And the backside of a Boa never stops –
Yet not one's got such a bottom as
The hugeous Hippopotamus.
For bottoms, Hippopotami are tops.

Dick King-Smith

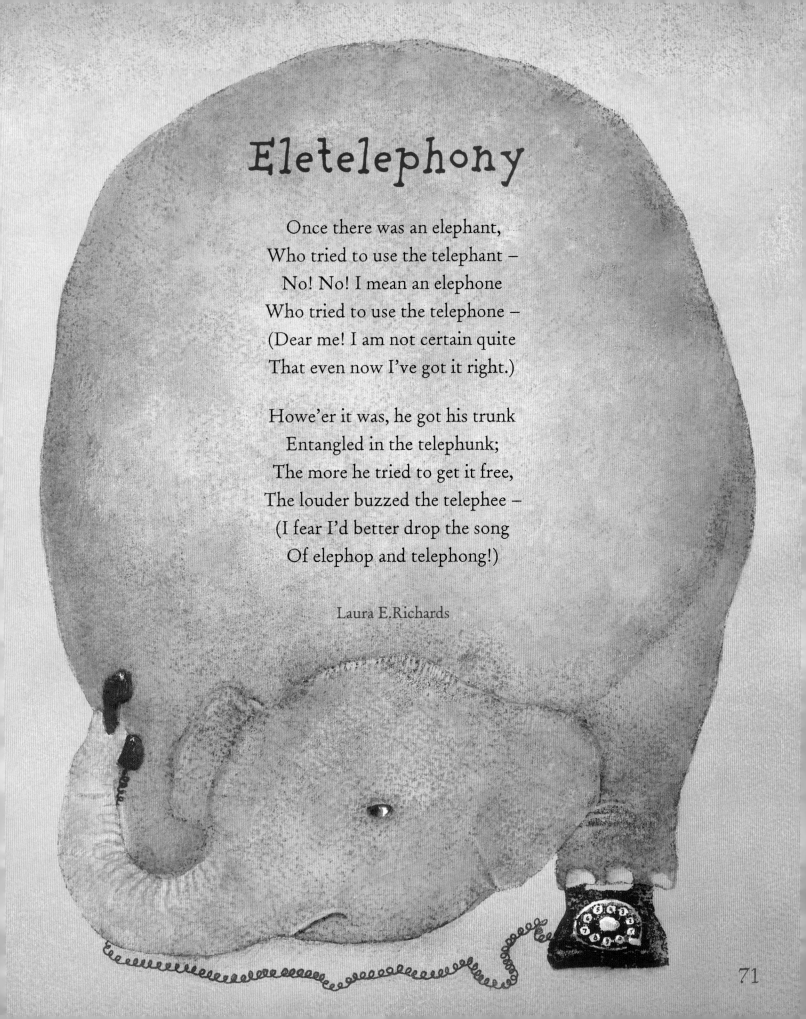

# Eletelephony

Once there was an elephant,
Who tried to use the telephant –
No! No! I mean an elephone
Who tried to use the telephone –
(Dear me! I am not certain quite
That even now I've got it right.)

Howe'er it was, he got his trunk
Entangled in the telephunk;
The more he tried to get it free,
The louder buzzed the telephee –
(I fear I'd better drop the song
Of elephop and telephong!)

Laura E.Richards

# Grannie

I stayed with her when I was six then went
To live elsewhere when I was eight years old.
For ages I remembered her faint scent
Of lavender, the way she'd never scold
No matter what I'd done, and most of all
The way her smile seemed, somehow, to enfold
My whole world like a warm, protective shawl.

I knew that I was safe when she was near,
She was so tall, so wide, so large, she would
Stand mountainous between me and my fear,
Yet oh, so gentle, and she understood
Every hope and dream I ever had.
She praised me lavishly when I was good,
But never punished me when I was bad.

Years later war broke out and I became
A soldier and was wounded while in France.
Back home in hospital, still very lame,
I realized suddenly that circumstance
Had brought me close to that small town where she
Was living still. And so I seized the chance
To write and ask if she could visit me.

She came. And I still vividly recall
The shock that I received when she appeared
That dark cold day. Huge grannie was so small!
A tiny, frail, old lady. It was weird.
She hobbled through the ward to where I lay
And drew quite close and, hesitating, peered.
And then she smiled: and love lit up the day.

Vernon Scannell

# The Mad Gardener's Song

He thought he saw an Elephant,
  That practised on a fife:
He looked again, and found it was
  A letter from his wife.
"At length I realise," he said,
  "The bitterness of Life!"

He thought he saw a Buffalo
  Upon the chimney-piece:
He looked again, and found it was
  His Sister's Husband's Niece.
"Unless you leave this house," he said,
  "I'll send for the Police!"

He thought he saw a Rattlesnake
  That questioned him in Greek:
He looked again, and found it was
  The Middle of Next Week.
"The one thing I regret," he said,
  "Is that it cannot speak!"

He thought he saw a Banker's Clerk
    Descending from the bus:
He looked again, and found it was
    A Hippopotamus:
"If this should stay to dine," he said,
    "There won't be much for us!"

He thought he saw a Kangaroo
    That worked a coffee-mill:
He looked again, and found it was
    A Vegetable-Pill.
"Were I to swallow this," he said,
    "I should be very ill!"

He thought he saw a Coach-and-Four
    That stood beside his bed:
He looked again, and found it was
    A Bear without a Head.
"Poor thing," he said, "poor silly thing!
    "It's waiting to be fed!"

He thought he saw an Albatross
   That fluttered round the lamp:
He looked again, and found it was
   A Penny-Postage-Stamp.
"You'd best be getting home," he said,
   "The nights are very damp!"

He thought he saw a Garden-Door
   That opened with a key:
He looked again, and found it was
   A Double Rule of Three:
"And all its mystery," he said,
   "Is clear as day to me!"

He thought he saw an Argument
   That proved he was the Pope:
He looked again, and found it was
   A Bar of Mottled Soap.
"A fact so dread," he faintly said,
   "Extinguishes all hope!"

Lewis Carroll

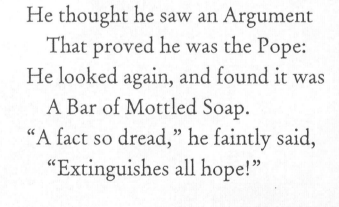

# Fame was a Claim of Uncle Ed's

Fame was a claim of Uncle Ed's,
Simply because he had three heads,
Which, if he'd only had a third of,
I think he would never have been heard of.

Ogden Nash

# from The Garden

What wondrous life is this I lead!
Ripe apples drop about my head;
The luscious clusters of the vine
Upon my mouth do crush their wine;
The nectarine and curious peach
Into my hands themselves do reach;
Stumbling on melons, as I pass,
Ensnared with flowers, I fall on grass.

Here at the fountain's sliding foot,
Or at some fruit-tree's mossy root,
Casting the body's vest aside,
My soul into the boughs does glide;
There, like a bird, it sits and sings,
Then whets and combs its silver wings,
And, till prepared for longer flight,
Waves in its plumes the various light.

Andrew Marvell

# The Day's Eye

The sun rises,
surprises the weary night,
like a sudden joke.
Daylight.

The sun gleams,
beams kindly heat
like an oven's plate.
Streets sweat.

The sun sneaks,
peeks through misty cloud,
like a sly thief,
alone in a crowd.

The sun sleeps,
creeps into cool shade,
like a honey cat.
Shadows fade.

The sun slips,
dips into night,
like a closing mouth,
swallowing light.

Pie Corbett

# The Dawn Wind

At two o'clock in the morning, if you open your window and listen,
  You will hear the feet of the Wind that is going to call the sun.
And the trees in the shadow rustle and the trees in the moonlight glisten,
  And though it is deep, dark night, you feel that the night is done.

So do the cows in the field. They graze for an hour and lie down,
  Dozing and chewing the cud; or a bird in the ivy wakes,
Chirrups one note and is still, and the restless Wind strays on,
  Fidgeting far down the road, till, softly, the darkness breaks.

Back comes the Wind full strength with a blow like an angel's wing,
  Gentle but waking the world, as he shouts: "The Sun! The Sun!"
And the light floods over the fields and the birds begin to sing,
  And the Wind dies down in the grass. It is day and his work is done.

So when the world is asleep, and there seems no hope of her waking
  Out of some long, bad dream that makes her mutter and moan,
Suddenly, all men arise to the noise of fetters breaking,
  And every one smiles at his neighbour and tells him his soul is his own!

Rudyard Kipling

# Out in the Dark

Out in the dark over the snow
The fallow fawns invisible go
With the fallow doe;
And the winds blow
Fast as the stars are slow.

Stealthily the dark haunts round
And, when the lamp goes, without sound
At a swifter bound
Than the swiftest hound,
Arrives, and all else is drowned.

And star and I and wind and deer
Are in the dark together, – near,
Yet far, – and fear
Drums on my ear
In that sage company drear.

How weak and little is the light,
All the universe of sight,
Love and delight,
Before the might,
If you love it not, of night.

Edward Thomas

# Speak of the North

Speak of the North! A lonely moor
Silent and dark and tractless swells,
The waves of some wild streamlet pour
Hurriedly through its ferny dells.

Profoundly still the twilight air,
Lifeless the landscape; so we deem
Till like a phantom gliding near
A stag bends down to drink the stream.

And far away a mountain zone,
A cold, white waste of snow-drifts lies,
And one star, large and soft and lone,
Silently lights the unclouded skies.

Charlotte Brontë

# The Secret Brother

Jack lived in the green-house
When I was six,
With glass and with tomato plants,
Not with slates and bricks.

I didn't have a brother,
Jack became mine.
Nobody could see him,
He never gave a sign.

Just beyond the rockery,
By the apple-tree,
Jack and his old mother lived,
Only for me.

With a tin telephone
Held beneath the sheet,
I would talk to Jack each night.
We would never meet.

Once my sister caught me,
Said, "He isn't there.
Down among the flower-pots
Cramm the gardener

Is the only person."
I said nothing, but
Let her go on talking.
Yet I moved Jack out.

He and his old mother
Did a midnight flit.
No one knew his number:
I had altered it.

Only I could see
The sagging washing-line
And my brother making
Our own secret sign.

Elizabeth Jennings

# Throwing a Tree

The two executioners stalk along over the knolls,
Bearing two axes with heavy heads shining and wide,
And a long limp two-handled saw toothed for cutting great boles,
And so they approach the proud tree that bears the death-mark on its side.

Jackets doffed they swing axes and chop away just above ground,
And the chips fly about and lie white on the moss and fallen leaves;
Till a broad deep gash in the bark is hewn all the way round,
And one of them tries to hook upward a rope, which at last he achieves.

The saw then begins, till the top of the tall giant shivers:
The shivers are seen to grow greater each cut than before:
They edge out the saw, tug the rope; but the tree only quivers,
And kneeling and sawing again, they step back to try pulling once more.

Then, lastly, the living mast sways, further sways: with a shout
Job and Ike rush aside. Reached the end of its long staying powers
The tree crashes downward: it shakes all its neighbours throughout,
And two hundred years' steady growth has been ended
in less than two hours.

Thomas Hardy

# The Shark

A treacherous monster is the Shark,
He never makes the least remark.

And when he sees you on the sand,
He doesn't seem to want to land.

He watches you take off your clothes,
And not the least excitement shows.

His eyes do not grow bright or roll,
He has astounding self-control.

He waits till you are quite undressed,
And seems to take no interest.

And when towards the sea you leap,
He looks as if he were asleep.

But when you once get in his range,
His whole demeanour seems to change.

He throws his body right about
And his true character comes out.

It's no use crying or appealing,
He seems to lose all decent feeling.

After this warning you will wish
To keep clear of this treacherous fish.

His back is black, his stomach white,
He has a very dangerous bite.

Lord Alfred Douglas

# When to the Sessions
# of Sweet Silent Thought

When to the sessions of sweet silent thought
I summon up remembrance of things past,
I sigh the lack of many a thing I sought,
And with old woes new wail my dear time's waste:
Then can I drown an eye, unused to flow,
For precious friends hid in death's dateless night,
And weep afresh love's long since cancelled woe,
And moan the expense of many a vanished sight:
Then can I grieve at grievances foregone,
And heavily from woe to woe tell o'er
The sad account of fore-bemoanèd moan,
Which I new pay as if not paid before.
   But if the while I think on thee, dear friend,
    All losses are restored and sorrows end.

William Shakespeare

# Friends

I fear it's very wrong of me
And yet I must admit
When someone offers friendship
I want the *whole* of it.
I don't want everybody else
To share my friends with me.
At least, I want *one* special one,
Who indisputably

Likes me much more than all the rest,
Who's always on my side,
Who never cares what others say,
Who lets me come and hide
Within his shadow, in his house –
It doesn't matter where –
Who lets me simply be myself,
Who's always, *always* there.

Elizabeth Jennings

# Wild Man Dancing

Between the ocean and the cliff,
He moves across the sand;
Head back, as if about to laugh,
And flailing like a fire in the wind.

His arms sweep wide, embracing air,
He rises on his toes,
He feints, he rushes here and there,
Then turns, and crouches low, and holds the pose.

Some distant walkers stop and frown,
But never think to ask
Why this old, half-naked clown
Is trying to be music in the dusk.

They stroll back to their nightly news,
But something passed them by:
His sun-flecked eyes that never lose
The small white kite he nurses round the sky.

Sam Taplin

# Colonel Fazackerley

Colonel Fazackerley Butterworth-Toast
Bought an old castle complete with a ghost,
But someone or other forgot to declare
To Colonel Fazack that the spectre was there.

On the very first evening, while waiting to dine,
The Colonel was taking a fine sherry wine,
When the ghost, with a furious flash and a flare,
Shot out of the chimney and shivered, "Beware!"

Colonel Fazackerley put down his glass
And said, "My dear fellow, that's really first class!
I just can't conceive how you do it at all.
I imagine you're going to a Fancy Dress Ball?"

At this, the dread ghost gave a withering cry.
Said the Colonel (his monocle firm in his eye),
"Now just how you do it I wish I could think.
Do sit down and tell me, and please have a drink."

The ghost in his phosphorous cloak gave a roar
And floated about between ceiling and floor.

He walked through a wall and returned through a pane
And backed up the chimney and came down again.

Said the Colonel, "With laughter I'm feeling quite weak!"
(As trickles of merriment ran down his cheek).
"My house-warming party I hope you won't spurn.
You *must* say you'll come and you'll give us a turn!"

At this, the poor spectre – quite out of his wits –
Proceeded to shake himself almost to bits.
He rattled his chains and he clattered his bones
And he filled the whole castle with mumbles and moans.

But Colonel Fazackerley, just as before,
Was simply delighted and called out, "Encore!"
At which the ghost vanished, his efforts in vain,
And never was seen at the castle again.

"Oh dear, what a pity!" said Colonel Fazack.
"I don't know his name, so I can't call him back."
And then with a smile that was hard to define,
Colonel Fazackerley went in to dine.

Charles Causley

# The Cow

The cow is of the bovine ilk;
One end is moo, the other milk.

Ogden Nash

# Weasel

The Weasel whizzes through the woods, he sizzles through the brambles,
Compared to him a rabbit hobbles and a whippet ambles.

He's all the heads of here and there, he spins you in a dither,
He's peering out of everywhere, his ten tails hither thither.

The Weasel never waits to wonder what it is he's after.
It's butchery he wants, and BLOOD, and merry belly laughter.

That's all, that's all, it's no good thinking he's a darling creature.
Weight for weight he's twice a tiger, which he'd like to teach you.

A lucky thing we're giants! It can't be very nice
Dodging from the Weasel down the mazes of the mice.


Ted Hughes

# The Snitterjipe

In mellow orchards, rich and ripe,
Is found the luminous Snitterjipe.
Bad boys who climb the bulging trees
Feel his sharp breath about their knees;
His trembling whiskers tickle so,
They squeak and squeal till they let go.
They hear his far-from-friendly bark;
They see his eyeballs in the dark
Shining and shifting in their sockets
As round and big as pears in pockets.
They feel his hot and wrinkly hide;
They see his nostrils flaming wide,
His tapering teeth, his jutting jaws,
His tongue, his tail, his twenty claws.

His hairy shadow in the moon,
It makes them sweat, it makes them swoon;
And as they climb the orchard wall,
They let their pilfered pippins fall.
The Snitterjipe suspends pursuit
And falls upon the fallen fruit;
And while they flee the monster fierce,
Apples, not boys, his talons pierce.
With thumping hearts they hear him munch –
Six apples at a time he'll crunch.
At length he falls asleep, and they
On tiptoe take their homeward way.
But long before the blackbirds pipe
To welcome day, the Snitterjipe
Has fled afar, and on the green
Only his fearsome prints are seen.

James Reeves

# Escape Plan

As I, Stegosaurus,
stand motionless
in the museum
I am secretly planning
My escape.

At noon
Tyrannosaurus Rex
will cause a diversion
by wheeling around the museum's high ceilings
and diving at the curators and museum staff
while I
quietly slip out of the fire exit
and melt
into the London crowds.

Roger Stevens

# Upon Westminster Bridge

Earth has not anything to show more fair:
Dull would he be of soul who could pass by
A sight so touching in its majesty:
This City now doth, like a garment, wear
The beauty of the morning; silent, bare,
Ships, towers, domes, theatres, and temples lie
Open unto the fields, and to the sky;
All bright and glittering in the smokeless air.

Never did sun more beautifully steep
In his first splendour, valley, rock, or hill;
Ne'er saw I, never felt, a calm so deep!
The river glideth at his own sweet will:
Dear God! the very houses seem asleep;
And all that mighty heart is lying still!

William Wordsworth

# The Months

January brings the snow,
Makes our feet and fingers glow.

February brings the rain,
Thaws the frozen lake again.

March brings breezes, loud and shrill,
To stir the dancing daffodil.

April brings the primrose sweet,
Scatters daisies at our feet.

May brings flocks of pretty lambs,
Skipping by their fleecy dams.

June brings tulips, lilies, roses,
Fills the children's hands with posies.

Hot July brings cooling showers,
Apricots and gillyflowers.

August brings the sheaves of corn,
Then the harvest home is borne.

Warm September brings the fruit,
Sportsmen then begin to shoot.

Fresh October brings the pheasant,
Then to gather nuts is pleasant.

Dull November brings the blast,
Then the leaves are whirling fast.

Chill December brings the sleet,
Blazing fire, and Christmas treat.

Sara Coleridge

# The Visitor

A crumbling churchyard, the sea and the moon;
The waves had gouged out grave and bone;
A man was walking, late and alone...

He saw a skeleton on the ground;
A ring on a bony hand he found.

He ran home to his wife and gave her the ring.
"Oh, where did you get it?" He said not a thing.

"It's the prettiest ring in the world," she said,
As it glowed on her finger. They skipped off to bed.

At midnight they woke. In the dark outside,
"Give me my ring!" a chill voice cried.

"What was that, William? What did it say?"
"Don't worry, my dear. It'll soon go away."

"I'm coming!" A skeleton opened the door.
  "Give me my ring!" It was crossing the floor.

  "What was that, William? What did it say?"
  "Don't worry, my dear. It'll soon go away."

  "I'm touching you now! I'm climbing the bed."
  The wife pulled the sheet right over her head.

It was torn from her grasp and tossed in the air:
  "I'll drag you out of your bed by the hair!"

  "What was that, William? What did it say?"
  "Throw the ring through the window! THROW IT AWAY!"

  She threw it. The skeleton leapt from the sill,
    Scooped up the ring and clattered downhill,
      Fainter...and fainter...Then all was still.

Ian Serraillier

# from The Lighthouse

The rocky ledge runs far into the sea,
And on its outer point, some miles away,
The Lighthouse lifts its massive masonry,
A pillar of fire by night, of cloud by day.

Even at this distance I can see the tides,
Upheaving, break unheard along its base,
A speechless wrath, that rises and subsides
In the white lip and tremor of the face.

And as the evening darkens, lo! how bright,
Through the deep purple of the twilight air,
Beams forth the sudden radiance of its light
With strange, unearthly splendor in the glare!

Not one alone: from each projecting cape
And perilous reef along the ocean's verge,
Starts into life a dim, gigantic shape,
Holding its lantern o'er the restless surge.

And the great ships sail outward and return,
Bending and bowing o'er the billowy swells,
And ever joyful as they see it burn,
They wave their silent welcomes and farewells.

Henry Wadsworth Longfellow

# Sea-Fever

I must go down to the seas again, to the lonely sea and the sky,
And all I ask is a tall ship and a star to steer her by,
And the wheel's kick and the wind's song and the white sail's shaking,
And a grey mist on the sea's face, and a grey dawn breaking.

I must go down to the seas again, for the call of the running tide
Is a wild call and a clear call that may not be denied;
And all I ask is a windy day with the white clouds flying,
And the flung spray and the blown spume, and the seagulls crying.

I must go down to the seas again, to the vagrant gypsy life,
To the gull's way and the whale's way where the wind's like a whetted knife;
And all I ask is a merry yarn from a laughing fellow-rover
And quiet sleep and a sweet dream when the long trick's over.

John Masefield

# Shall I Compare Thee to a Summer's Day?

Shall I compare thee to a summer's day?
Thou art more lovely and more temperate:
Rough winds do shake the darling buds of May,
And summer's lease hath all too short a date:
Sometimes too hot the eye of heaven shines,
And often is his gold complexion dimmed;
And every fair from fair sometimes declines,
By chance or nature's changing course untrimmed;
But thy eternal summer shall not fade,
Nor lose possession of that fair thou owest,
Nor shall Death brag thou wanderest in his shade,
When in eternal lines to time thou growest:
So long as men can breathe, or eyes can see,
So long lives this, and this gives life to thee.

William Shakespeare

# She Walks in Beauty like the Night

She walks in beauty, like the night
Of cloudless climes and starry skies;
And all that's best of dark and bright
Meet in her aspect and her eyes:
Thus mellowed to that tender light
Which heaven to gaudy day denies.

One shade the more, one ray the less,
Had half impaired the nameless grace
Which waves in every raven tress,
Or softly lightens o'er her face;
Where thoughts serenely sweet express
How pure, how dear their dwelling-place.

And on that cheek, and o'er that brow,
So soft, so calm, yet eloquent,
The smiles that win, the tints that glow,
But tell of days in goodness spent,
A mind at peace with all below,
A heart whose love is innocent.

Lord Byron

# The Pelican Chorus

King and Queen of the Pelicans we;
No other Birds so grand we see!
None but we have feet like fins!
With lovely leathery throats and chins!
    Ploffskin, Pluffskin, Pelican jee!
    We think no Birds so happy as we!
    Plumpskin, Ploshkin, Pelican jill!
    We think so then, and we thought so still!

We live on the Nile. The Nile we love.
By night we sleep on the cliffs above;
By day we fish, and at eve we stand
On long bare islands of yellow sand.
And when the sun sinks slowly down
And the great rock walls grow dark and brown,
And the purple river rolls fast and dim,
And the ivory Ibis starlike skim,
Wing to wing we dance around,
Stamping our feet with a flumpy sound,
Opening our mouths as Pelicans ought,

And this is the song we nightly snort;
    Ploffskin, Pluffskin, Pelican jee!
    We think no Birds so happy as we!
    Plumpskin, Ploshkin, Pelican jill!
    We think so then, and we thought so still!

Last year came out our daughter, Dell;
And all the Birds received her well.
To do her honour, a feast we made
For every bird that can swim or wade.
Herons and Gulls, and Cormorants black,
Cranes, and Flamingoes with scarlet back,
Plovers and Storks, and Geese in clouds,
Swans and Dilberry Ducks in crowds.

Thousands of Birds in wondrous flight!
They ate and drank and danced all night,
And echoing back from the rocks you heard
Multitude-echoes from Bird and Bird,
    Ploffskin, Pluffskin, Pelican jee!
    We think no Birds so happy as we!
    Plumpskin, Ploshkin, Pelican jill!
    We think so then, and we thought so still!

Yes, they came; and among the rest,
The King of the Cranes all grandly dressed.
Such a lovely tail! Its feathers float
Between the ends of his blue dress-coat;
With pea-green trousers all so neat,
And a delicate frill to hide his feet,
(For though no one speaks of it, every one knows,
He has got no webs between his toes!)

As soon as he saw our Daughter Dell,
In violent love that Crane King fell,
On seeing her waddling form so fair,
With a wreath of shrimps in her short white hair,
And before the end of the next long day,
Our Dell had given her heart away;
For the King of the Cranes had won that heart,
With a Crocodile's egg and a large fish-tart.

She vowed to marry the King of the Cranes,
Leaving the Nile for stranger plains;
And away they flew in a gathering crowd
Of endless birds in a lengthening cloud.

Ploffskin, Pluffskin, Pelican jee!
We think no Birds so happy as we!
Plumpskin, Ploshkin, Pelican jill!
We think so then, and we thought so still!

And far away in the twilight sky,
We heard them singing a lessening cry,
Farther and farther till out of sight,
And we stood alone in the silent night!
Often since, in the nights of June,
We sit on the sand and watch the moon;
She has gone to the great Gromboolian plain,
And we probably never shall meet again!
Oft, in the long still nights of June,
We sit on the rocks and watch the moon;
 – She dwells by the streams of the Chankly Bore,
And we probably never shall see her more.
      Ploffskin, Pluffskin, Pelican jee!
      We think no Birds so happy as we!
      Plumpskin, Ploshkin, Pelican jill!
      We think so then, and we thought so still!

Edward Lear

# He Wishes for the Cloths of Heaven

Had I the heavens' embroidered cloths,
Enwrought with golden and silver light,
The blue and the dim and the dark cloths
Of night and light and the half-light,
I would spread the cloths under your feet:
But I, being poor, have only my dreams;
I have spread my dreams under your feet:
Tread softly because you tread on my dreams.

W.B.Yeats

# When You are Old and Grey

When you are old and grey and full of sleep,
And nodding by the fire, take down this book,
And slowly read, and dream of the soft look
Your eyes had once, and of their shadows deep;

How many loved your moments of glad grace,
And loved your beauty with love false or true,
But one man loved the pilgrim Soul in you,
And loved the sorrows of your changing face;

And bending down beside the glowing bars,
Murmur, a little sadly, how Love fled
And paced upon the mountains overhead
And hid his face amid a crowd of stars.

W.B.Yeats

# The Harvest Moon

The flame-red moon, the harvest moon,
Rolls along the hills, gently bouncing,
A vast balloon,
Till it takes off, and sinks upward
To lie on the bottom of the sky, like a gold doubloon.

The harvest moon has come,
Booming softly through heaven, like a bassoon.
And the earth replies all night, like a deep drum.

So people can't sleep,
So they go out where elms and oak trees keep
A kneeling vigil, in a religious hush.
The harvest moon has come!

And all the moonlit cows and all the sheep
Stare up at her petrified, while she swells
Filling heaven, as if red hot, and sailing
Closer and closer like the end of the world.

Till the gold fields of stiff wheat
Cry "We are ripe, reap us!" and the rivers
Sweat from the melting hills.

Ted Hughes

# To a Fish

You strange, astonished-looking, angle-faced,
Dreary-mouthed, gaping wretches of the sea,
Gulping salt water everlastingly,
Cold-blooded, though with red your blood be graced,
And mute, though dwellers in the roaring waste;
And you, all shapes beside, that fishy be, —
Some round, some flat, some long, all devilry,
Legless, unloving, infamously chaste: —

O scaly, slippery, wet, swift, staring wights,
What is it you do? What life lead? Eh, dull goggles?
How do you vary your vile days and nights?
How pass your Sundays? Are you still but joggles
In ceaseless wash? Still nought but gapes, and bites,
And drinks, and stares, diversified with boggles?

# A Fish Answers

Amazing monster! that, for all I know,
With the first sight of thee did make our race
Forever stare! O flat and shocking face,
Grimly divided from the breast below!
Thou that on dry land horribly dost go
With a split body and most ridiculous pace,
Prong after prong, disgracer of all grace,
Long-useless-finned, haired, upright, unwet, slow!

O breather of unbreathable, sword-sharp air,
How canst exist? How bear thyself, thou dry
And dreary sloth? What particle canst share
Of the only blessed life, the watery?
I sometimes see of you an actual *pair*
Go by! linked fin by fin, most odiously.

Leigh Hunt

# Do Not go Gentle into That Good Night

Do not go gentle into that good night,
Old age should burn and rave at close of day;
Rage, rage against the dying of the light.

Though wise men at their end know dark is right,
Because their words had forked no lightning, they
Do not go gentle into that good night.

Good men, the last wave by, crying how bright
Their frail deeds might have danced in a green bay,
Rage, rage against the dying of the light.

Wild men who caught and sang the sun in flight,
And learn, too late, they grieved it on its way,
Do not go gentle into that good night.

Grave men, near death, who see with blinding sight
Blind eyes could blaze like meteors and be gay,
Rage, rage against the dying of the light.

And you, my father, there on the sad height,
Curse, bless, me now with your fierce tears I pray.
Do not go gentle into that good night.
Rage, rage against the dying of the light.


Dylan Thomas

# Index of First Lines

# Index of Poets

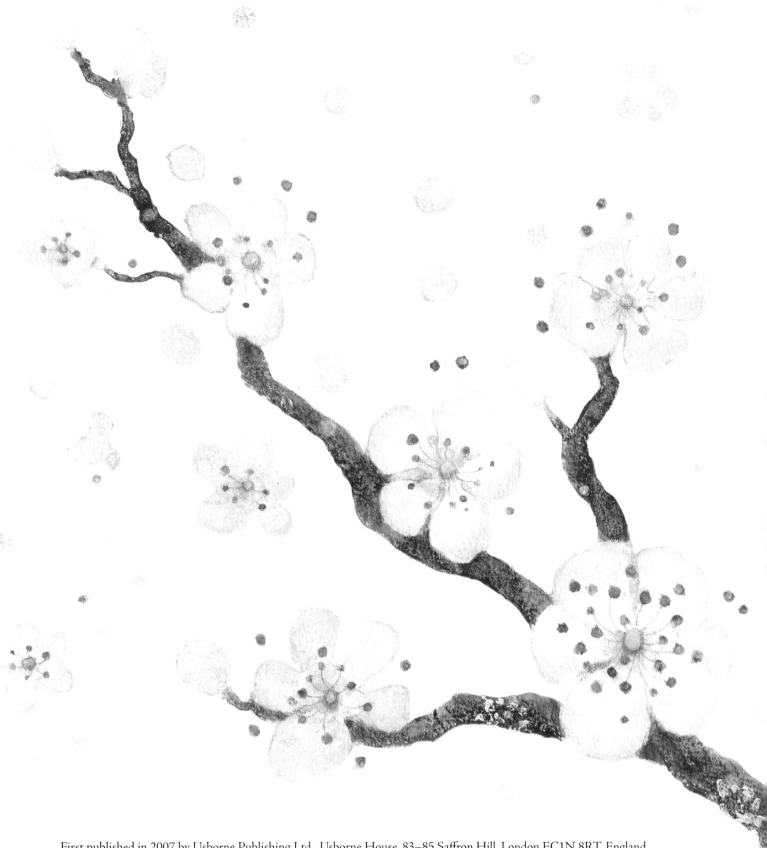

First published in 2007 by Usborne Publishing Ltd., Usborne House, 83–85 Saffron Hill, London EC1N 8RT, England.
This collection copyright ©2007 Usborne Publishing Ltd. The name Usborne and the devices 🎈 🎈 are Trade Marks of Usborne Publishing Ltd.
All rights reserved. No part of this publication may be reproduced, stored in a retrieval system, or transmitted in any form or by any means,
electronic, mechanical, photocopying, recording or otherwise without the prior permission of the publisher.
U.E. First published in America 2008. Printed in China.

# Acknowledgements

Every effort has been made to trace the copyright holders of the material in this book. If any rights have been omitted, the publishers offer to rectify this in any subsequent editions following notification. The publishers are grateful to the following individuals and organizations for their permission to reproduce copyright material.

14 "The Purist" by Ogden Nash. Copyright © (1936) Ogden Nash. Reprinted by permission of Curtis Brown, Ltd. Also from a book entitled "Candy is Dandy: The Best of Ogden Nash". Reprinted by permission of Andre Deutsch. 15 "Song sung by a Man on a Barge to Another Man on a Different Barge in order to drive him Mad" by Kit Wright. From HOT DOG AND OTHER POEMS by Kit Wright (Kestrel, 1981). Copyright © Kit Wright, 1981. 17 "Moonlit apples" by John Drinkwater. Reprinted by permission of Samuel French Ltd. on behalf of the Estate of John Drinkwater. 18 "The Day that Summer Died" by Vernon Scannell. Reprinted by permission of the author. 20 "The Hen" by Lord Alfred Douglas. Reprinted by courtesy of John Rubinstein and John Stratford (c) The Literary Executors of the Lord Alfred Douglas dec.d. All rights reserved. 21 "The Duck" by Lord Alfred Douglas. Reprinted by courtesy of John Rubinstein and John Stratford (c) The Literary Executors of the Lord Alfred Douglas dec.d. All rights reserved. 21 "The Nonny" by James Reeves. © James Reeves, 1960, from Prefabulous Animiles, published by E.P.Dutton. Reprinted by permission of the James Reeves Estate. 22 "Stopping by Woods on a Snowy Evening" by Robert Frost. From THE POETRY OF ROBERT FROST edited by Edward Connery Lathem. Copyright 1923, 1969 by Henry Holt and Company. Copyright 1951 by Robert Frost. Reprinted by permission of Henry Holt and Company, LLC. Also published by Jonathan Cape in the UK and reprinted by permission of The Random House Group Ltd. 24 "The Word Party" by Richard Edwards, from "The Word Party", published by Lutterworth Press. Reprinted by permission of the author. 25 "Words I Like" by Steve Turner. From The Day I Fell Down the Toilet by Steven Turner, published by Lion Hudson plc, 1996. Copyright © 1996 Steven Turner. Used with permission of Lion Hudson plc. 27 "The Magic Box" by Kit Wright. Reprinted by permission of the author. 29 "Out in the Desert" by Charles Causley, from Collected Poems for Children by Charles Causley, published by Macmillan Children's Books. Reprinted by permission of David Higham Associates. 31 "An April Sunday Brings the Snow" by Philip Larkin, from Collected Poems by Philip Larkin. Copyright © 1988, 2003 by The Estate of Philip Larkin. Reprinted by permission of Faber and Faber Limited and Farrar, Straus & Giroux LLC. 32 "The Cod" by Lord Alfred Douglas. Reprinted by courtesy of John Rubinstein and John Stratford (c) The Literary Executors of the Lord Alfred Douglas dec.d. All rights reserved. 33 "The Emergensea" by John Hegley. © 1995 John Hegley. Reprinted by permission of PFD on behalf of the author. 36 "Geography Lesson" by Brian Patten. © Brian Patten, c/o Rogers, Coleridge and White, 20 Powis Mews, London W11 1JN. 40 "A Small Dragon" by Brian Patten © Brian Patten, c/o Rogers, Coleridge and White, 20 Powis Mews, London W11 1JN. 42 "The Adventures of Isabel" by Ogden Nash. Copyright © (1936) by Ogden Nash. Reprinted by permission of Curtis Brown, Ltd. Also from a book entitled "Candy is Dandy: The Best of Ogden Nash". Reprinted by permission of Andre Deutsch. 44 "Mountains" by Ian Serraillier. From The Sun Goes Free (Longman, 1977). © Estate of Ian Serraillier. 46 "Limerick" by John Irwin. Reprinted by kind permission of Helen Irwin. 47 "Clerihew" by Roger McGough (Copyright © Roger McGough 1987) is reproduced by permission of PFD (www.pfd.co.uk) on behalf of Roger McGough. 53 "The Uncertainty of the Poet" by Wendy Cope. Copyright © Wendy Cope 1992. From Serious Concerns by Wendy Cope. Published by Faber & Faber, 1992. Reprinted by permission of PFD on behalf of the author. 55 "Flowers" by Wendy Cope. Copyright © Wendy Cope 1992. From Serious Concerns by Wendy Cope. Published by Faber & Faber, 1992. Reprinted by permission of PFD on behalf of the author. 59 "Night Football with my Brother" by Sam Taplin. Reproduced by permission of the author. 60 "A Liking for the Viking" by Celia Warren. First published in Vikings Don't Wear Pants, Roger Stevens and Celia Warren, KEP, 2001. © Celia Warren 2001. 61 "Roman Invasions" by Celia Warren. First published in Vikings Don't Wear Pants, Roger Stevens and Celia Warren, KEP, 2001. © Celia Warren 2001. 70 "Look back in wonder" by Dick King-Smith, by permission of A.P. Watt Ltd. on behalf of Fox Busters Ltd. 71 "Eletelephony" by Laura E. Richards from TIRRA LIRRA by Laura Richards. Copyright © 1930, 1932 by Laura E. Richards; Copyright © renewed 1960 by Hamilton Richards. By permission of Little, Brown and Co., Inc. 72 "Grannie" by Vernon Scannell. Reprinted by permission of the author. 77 "Fame was a Claim of Uncle Ed's" by Ogden Nash Copyright © (1953) by Ogden Nash. Reprinted by permission of Curtis Brown, Ltd. Also from a book entitled "Candy is Dandy: The Best of Ogden Nash". Reprinted by permission of Andre Deutsch. 80 "The Day's Eye" by Pie Corbett. Reprinted by permission of the author. 84 "The Secret Brother" by Elizabeth Jennings. From The Secret Brother by Elizabeth Jennings, published by Macmillan. Reprinted by permission of David Higham Associates. 88 "The Shark" by Lord Alfred Douglas. Reprinted by courtesy of John Rubinstein and John Stratford (c) The Literary Executors of the Lord Alfred Douglas dec. d. All rights reserved. 91 "Friends" by Elizabeth Jennings. From The Secret Brother by Elizabeth Jennings, published by Macmillan. Reprinted by permission of David Higham Associates. 92 "Wild Man Dancing" by Sam Taplin. Reproduced by permission of the author. 94 "Colonel Fazackerley" by Charles Causley. From Collected Poems for Children by Charles Causley, published by Macmillan Children's Books. Reprinted by permission of David Higham Associates. 96 "The Cow" by Ogden Nash Copyright © (1931) by Ogden Nash. Reprinted by permission of Curtis Brown, Ltd. Also from a book entitled "Candy is Dandy: The Best of Ogden Nash". Reprinted by permission of Andre Deutsch. 97 "Weasel" by Ted Hughes, from Collected Poems for Children by Ted Hughes, pictures by Raymond Briggs. Text copyright © 2005 by The Estate of Ted Hughes. Pictures copyright © 2005 by Raymond Briggs. Reprinted by permission of Faber and Faber Limited and Farrar, Straus & Giroux LLC. 99 "The Snitterjipe" by James Reeves © from COMPLETE POEMS FOR CHILDREN (HEINEMANN). Reprinted by permission of the James Reeves Estate. 101 "Escape Plan" by Roger Stevens. From The Monster That Ate the Universe by Roger Stevens (Macmillan Children's Books, 2004). © Roger Stevens. 106 "The Visitor" by Ian Serraillier. From A Second Book of Poetry (OUP, 1980). © Estate of Ian Serraillier. 109 "Sea-Fever" by John Masefield. Reprinted by permission of the Society of Authors as the Literary Representative of the Estate of John Masefield. 116 "He wishes for the Cloths of Heaven" by W. B. Yeats. By permission of A.P. Watt Ltd. on behalf of Gráinne Yeats. 117 "When You are Old and Grey" by W. B. Yeats. By permission of Scribner and A.P. Watt Ltd. on behalf of Gráinne Yeats. 118 "The Harvest Moon" by Ted Hughes, from Collected Poems by Ted Hughes. Copyright © 2003 by The Estate of Ted Hughes. Reprinted by permission of Faber and Faber Limited and Farrar, Straus & Giroux LLC. 122 "Do Not Go Gentle Into That Good Night" by Dylan Thomas, from THE POEMS OF DYLAN THOMAS, copyright ©1952 by Dylan Thomas, Reprinted by permission of New Directions Publishing Corp. Also from "Collected poems" by Dylan Thomas, published by Dent. Reprinted by permission of David Higham Associates.
Cover design by Claire Ever and Matt Durber. Additional design by Meg Dobbie.